Impressions Indelible

A kaleidoscope of experiences

Madhu K. Sarao

BookLeaf Publishing

India | USA | UK

Made with ❤ on the BookLeaf Publishing Platform
www.bookleafpub.in
www.bookleafpub.com

Dedication

I dedicate this book to my Guru, who has been my constant and biggest source of strength. His grace nudged me to venture into areas unknown to me before. His powerful and golden words made me believe in myself and never left me alone in this journey.

Preface

'Impressions Indelible' is a collection of poems based on years of my worldly experience. Each piece is an outpouring of a suppressed emotion finding an outlet through the medium of poetry. This book is a fusion of bitter, sweet and sour experiences.

Acknowledgements

I express my heartfelt gratitude to my daughter, without whose support, thoughts would have remained thoughts and not taken a tangible form.

1. Your Hand
(To my Guru)

When you came into my life one day
I knew it was something important to convey
I could never have asked for anything more
I am ever and ever thankful to you from the core

Oh, my Saviour! How long have you made me wait
I wish you had come into my life, not so late
My life was in chaos and turmoil and pain
When you came I realized my struggle did not go in vain

You filled me with hope; you taught me to dream
Your grace has filled, to the brim, my dry stream
Your unconditional love and patience are a boon
Which in my life will always be there like a moon

Oh! How in my darkest moods you stood like a rock
And silently watched over me, lifting me from shock
I want to thank you and thank you forever
My life is never going to be the same ever

2. Never Mind (Words of courage and hope)

Never mind if you are crushed
For it's a chance to simply get up

Never mind if there is darkness
Struggle, because you can always find light

Never mind if you are betrayed
It's a chance you can still pray

Never mind if you are the butt of jokes
You can still manage to focus on your goals

Never mind if barbs of criticism are thrown
Come out and explore the ways unknown

Never mind if the going is tough
You can still find shades to rest

Never mind if tears are rolling down
Remember after the suffering there is a crown

Never mind if the sun hasn't shone
You can always make a cozy bed alone

Never mind if muddy water is splashed on you
How strong you are even you don't have a clue

3. Solitude
(Cherished moments)

I cherish the moments when I am alone
They fill me with happiness more than before
Every time I spot a corner, I am by my own
In these heavenly moments I feel so secure

Blessed are those who have caring company
But for me my solitude and I are important the most
No matter how, I easily tune in with my own symphony
In such special moments, past memories come like
ghosts

Bygones are bygones I know; so why let them bother?
When I realize this, immediately I ask them to go
Instead, I dwell on something which does not smother
I feel so free and fly like a cloud with no pomp and show

These moments are heavenly blessings I am sure
The cares of the world don't bother me any more
I drift into the unknown and feel so free and light
My heartbeat silences and makes my little world bright

4. Pain
(Losing a loved one)

When you left, I got bereft of my sanity
I thought I lost it all as you were my everything

I can still recall the pain that made me numb
Dazed and so weak! I had no clue why it was me
What was it so grave; an answer to it I still crave

You were my sunshine; an important part of my life
Growing up together; saying so much without saying
Feeling each other's pain; what did you gain?

I remember your warmth; your presence lit
Every atom of mine; as you were my sunshine
I prayed for you; I looked up to you

The love we share is deep I still feel
It will stand the test of time
Passing the test of time the wound will heal

Where have you gone? Why have you gone?
The answer to this only you know; I do
Wish that we come together to be forever again

5. If I Were A Flying Cloud (Cherishing freedom)

If I were a flying cloud I would float around
Feeling the wind in my atoms, with happiness new found
I would pass over trees; I would pass over mountains
With boundless happiness; it would be as good as it sounds

I would have no time to care about
The mundane activities of the day
I would be the king and would bow to none
Enjoying life like a child on the run

If I saw a tear running down a cheek
I would extend my hand to wipe it instantly
Life would be surreal when nothing would
Come in the way of carrying the burden of many and throwing it away

I would be in the company of stars, twinkling all the way
In my quest to know them more, I would linger on my stay
The fairies and the angels would ride on my back

In that world where nothing is black

Oh! How I wish to escape the noise
To the world where peace is the only choice
Time would stop, bringing an end,
To all the worthless pursuits and with infinity, I would
blend

6. Brave Hearts
(Salute to the fighting spirit
of men)

I saw a man knee deep in water
Carrying a kettle of tea, making me
Wonder, what on earth is his purpose
He pointed out to a bunch of men
With axes and brooms in their hands
'To them I am taking tea-those sons of God

The whole land was submerged in water
Crisis looming large; tragedy had struck
With prayers in the heart, the people of the
Land gathered as one, holding each others'
Hands, not letting their spirit dampen
'It's God's will', with folded hands, they said

The news spread, far and wide, and
The sons of the soil - brave hearts, stood
Up like a back bone, pledging not to
Leave the suffering ones, till the end, by
Being on their side - if this is the spirit
Of these men, then recovery cannot be withheld

It is not that only the sons of the soil wept
On seeing the plight of the old and the young
Tears rolled down the cheeks of the
Other country men; seeing the helplessness
Of everyone they rose for their
Brothers - for such is the heart of men

We must learn a lesson from every stroke of nature
Even if it is harsh, bear it in your heart
That every time you fall - you don't fall to perish
It is the strength that is in you, that needs to be
awakened
When there is nothing left - that is the time,
Mind you - that is the time, to write a new chapter

7. Beware
(Hypocrisy at its best)

Beware of sweet words and smiling faces
For they are foxes in the guise of molasses
They will never let you know their true motive
But they will surely pretend that they are supportive

Beware of those who claim to be hardworking
For they show their true colors when the time comes
asking
All their tall claims fail when they wail
They have been targeted; Injustice indeed prevails!

Beware of those who talk about empathy and showcase
duality
They are the ones who show ruthlessness and cruelty
What to talk of their aggression when it comes to
calculation
They can give you a run for your money if you challenge
their devotion

Acting like foxes and snakes they take inspiration from
nature
Acting polished and refined they think there is none to
match their stature

The values they endorse are impossible to emulate
God, save the rest of the lot, from the rules they
formulate

8. My Mother
(Mothers are mothers)

Wise, intelligent and sharp is my mother
Who keeps losing everyday something or the other
When she thinks she has counted the money
She keeps it aside till she finds the money missing
She raises an uproar in the house wishing somebody
puts it back without a sound

It is her queer way of finding things
Blaming the maid for losing a thing
She shares the secret with her pride unhidden
That makes me laugh but hurting a little

She keeps us on toes for her perfection so dear
That makes us fumble even if things are clear
She will go on sewing till she feels
With spectacles on her nose forgetting her meals

Ever ready to go for outings no matter what
I asked her if she ever gets hurt......
Her strength and zeal for life is exceptional
I am grateful to her for being so unconditional

9. Embracing The Unknown (Trust your instinct)

A wise old man once asked,
"Do you know the key to surpass
The challenges that lie your path
With grace and poise, remaining unscathed?

Among the crowd a hand came up
Of a young monk who said, "It is so
easy sir, to surpass any difficulty that
life throws at us, remaining unscathed.

What is it tell me fast, for I am eager
to know who knows it all!
Sir, the key is to always take the beaten path
Avoiding the risk of the unknown and mysterious paths

How will that, my son, ensure your success?
When each one of us need a different mind set to
progress
The truth is that, the wise old man said,
'You can't go ahead till you embrace the unknown like a
long lost friend'.

Come what may your preparedness will not stay

In the time of crisis the only thing which may
Come to your rescue is keeping your ego at bay
And jumping into the fray, trusting your instinct, come
what may

10. Silence

(My strongest wish)

In the deep recesses of my mind
A strong wish is seeded, not for
Fame, not for money but for something
Which I value the great

Beyond the chatter of the world
beyond the chatter of the mind
I nourish my wish all the time with longing
And devotion hoping for a better time

No way can the storm bring me down
I am made of the toughest steel
And know how to shine
For the sun is my saviour in whose warmth I resign

Countless times the tug of war was won by the mind
Making me wonder if I could ever come out from the
pain of this kind
Terrified, I thought, if that was the end of life
Only to be revived by the deep touch of the divine

I crave for silence so profound and deep
That I need no one to disturb my peace

Not even the seemingly impossible tasks
Can bother me with their burden on me

I want that peace which connects me with the real me
Other wise futile are such efforts
That take me away from my real me
And I can never let that be

11. Gratitude
(You owe it to your parents)

You owe it to your parents
For the untiring efforts
They have made in raising you

The silent prayers with tears in eyes
When you appeared for exams or had been hospitalized
The countless sacrifices tell a tale
Of those who have braved all odds till they could make

Don't take them wrong for the mistakes they make
For they have been raised in a certain way
It's a pity that when they break, there is no one to
console them or take their pain
The pain which has always been there

Who is to be blamed - your upbringing or theirs?
The world will be as it has always been - full of
restraints, expectations, madness and noise
In this clamour called life; take a while and think of
peace, not of strife

You have to give it back one day - everything that you
have of privilege

One by one all the blessings that came your way
Because of your parents who raised you day by day
A heart full of gratitude can never betray!

12. My Country
(I am rooted to my country)

The sun shines brighter on my land
And the night sky boasts of a grand
Canvas of dimly lit stars and a moon
Which shines perfectly spelling a boon

The picturesque setting of the night
Of my land is a heart warming sight
I have grown up looking with eyes
Full of longing at the promising skies

Everything of my land, my country I
Cherish; the Himalayas touching the sky
The rays of the sun that makes the day bright
Receding like waves of the ocean at night

The fusion of the rich and the poor
Thronging the temples with the faith that binds
Not to forget the joy of togetherness that is witnessed
When the country plays with devotion and the opponent
leaves distressed

The festive spirit, that grips and makes
My country the best of all, is what it takes

To make it great, and a place to revere!
It just takes love for all differences to clear

I bow down to the land of saints and sages
Who have protected its people for ages and ages
This is something that the world must learn
Or else the fire of ego and power might burn

My country is my identity, my pride
I may sleep hungry, with only prayers by my side
But I will always feel safe in the arms of my motherland
Because there will be no one to say "leave our land"

13. The Wind
(Nature - my companion forever)

I want to kiss the wind
The whispering of whom
Tells me the secret to bloom

I want to embrace the wind
For I know in its soft touch
I will never be alone

I want to be caressed by the wind
Because in its each loving caress
I will find blessings manifold

The wind is my mother who is
Always by my side and in whose bosom
Lies all my secrets safe

When I stand with open arms
Letting it pass through me, it
Touches me giving me strength again

O Mother Nature, I bow down to you

The omnipresent, the all - pervading
I want to be ever protected by you

14. Let The Clouds Pass
(Learn to overcome sadness)

When heavily laden dark clouds float
Making you numb and shaking to the core
Then you remember words the wise men wrote:
"Let the clouds pass to see what is in store"

Your worries come like a passing phase
Not to stay but only to test and raise
The human being in you, prodding you more and more
Let the clouds pass to see what is in store

With tears unstoppable and the heart about to burst
And the only thing the mind says, "This is the worst"
Then close your eyes and delve deep in the core
Let the clouds pass to see what is in store

When the clouds of self doubt loom large
And there is no way light can barge
Into the corners of the mind - then what more?
Let the clouds pass to see what is in store

Be thankful that you are not alone and are alive
In the maze of life the rule is to strife and survive
Choosing never to look back on the chapter you tore

Let the clouds pass to see what is in store

15. Barren Land
(The power of nature)

The land that I walk upon
Is a barren land; drawn
Like a painting, still and silent
Unquestionably once a place, non-violent

Every grain of sand, every dry bush
Which I can see far and wide
Calls upon me to sit by their side
And listen to the story of their pride

The barren land was not barren then
It stood proud with its cheerful women and
hardworking men
The crops in the lush green fields
Danced to the lilting tunes, that healed

The peacocks and sparrows once ruled
And the clear sparkling waters cooled
Infants with chubby cheeks and twinkling eyes
Sent peals of laughter into the skies

Boys and girls played to their heart's content
And the fairies followed wherever they went

From dawn till dusk with activities rife
Everybody lived a life that knew no strife

Then what happened no one can guess
Their world came crashing down into a mess
The angry waters with a sinister smile
Engulfed the land, at night - so hostile!

The raging waters gave no warning
And stealthily swept away everything by the morning
To tell the tale there was just a single soul alive
Agony written large on his face, it was difficult to thrive

It was a ghastly sight and difficult to behold
He mustered strength, controlling the tears that rolled
And with one last look that drove him insane
He moved on making no attempt to look back again

As I walk upon the barren land which once thrived
I look at the clear blue sky spread far and wide
In the larger scheme of things that nature designs
I know I have no power and nothing is mine

16. An Ode to a Flower (Spreading happiness)

Swaying in the breeze lightly, you invite
The colourful butterflies, that make a lovely sight
Gently touching the velvety petals, they land
Like an angel, ticking softly, on your soft hand

Blooming in the sun and in the rain alike
Spreading your fragrance, whatever the weather be like
In hues of different kinds, you touch so many lives
For a child, who holds you tight, you are a wonder

For someone in love, you are a hope, and make them
ponder
If luck favours them or not; and surely for leaders
You are a parameter, deciding their success
From the number of garlands they possess

You look nice on the last ride
Of someone who has died
At God's feet, on birthday wishes, for every occasion
You are the reason for delight- being God's own creation

17. Night
(Integral part of life)

Night is the time that I crave
Like a blanket it surrounds me to save
From the doubts and frustrations that are grave
Which it puts to rest, pulling me out of the cave

Looking at the still night sky
Painted with a crescent-shaped moon, I sigh
Marvelling at its golden beauty against the vastness of
the night sky
I make a wish for it to be always there with a smile

It talks in loud whispers that only I can hear
And, strangely, gives me strength in a way
Making me wonder the power it possesses to clear
The mind of all clutter, that I could only pray

Unfathomable is the magic of the night
It can rip apart the heart of the sinner, turning it white
In its folds, the night holds, sights so bright
And an awakening which only a few achieve with their
might

18. Spare Them Please!
(Grooming the young)

Spare them please, spare them of your love and care
I mean the young - let them bloom
And find their way without your say

O teachers, don't become preachers
You know nothing till you have experimented
Just passing on the information, is not the game
You are the chosen ones, realize that, then act

O teachers, don't mind that I remind that
You yourself are learners all your life
Show them the way, become torch bearers
Don't demand a fan base, spare them of your
Love and care; spare a thought for the poor lot

'Catch them young' is a beautiful way
To dump on them, trash, as they have no say
Spare a thought for the poor lot; don't let them rot
Teach them how to think, let them not sink
 From where it is difficult to rise up again

Don't corrode their minds; don't teach them to spy
Remember what you give, you will have to receive

Then don't crib because you had asked for it
Your performance oriented approach can harm
Teach them how to stand on their feet

It's an appeal become a partner in their dreams
Be a pillar to them and lend your support
To build their self belief; then see them grow
With unadulterated minds, happy and gay
Leaving the whole world behind without anybody's say

19. My Inspiration (My pillar of strength - making my will to live stronger)

To every breath and whiff of air
That I feel, I have to admit, I owe
To a greater force, by virtue of its care
My day and night are secure, I know

Every morsel is a blessing from above
Every morning is another day of love
A chance to celebrate life once more
If you know you will be grateful to the core

The peacocks dancing after the rain
Bring a joy that cannot be explained
Who to owe these beautiful sights?
I wonder, on my solitary walks, at nights

The open grasslands and the desert lands
The beauty of it all makes the earth grand
 Deep is the inspiration for me to ignore

I fall, I rise, I fall again till it hurts no more

20. Nature
(My heart's longing to be in its company)

It fills my heart with pleasure when in company with nature
It simply raises my spirits and fills my eyes with brightness
There is no longing left and no desire when greenery all around I admire
The pristine, out of the world landscapes that I see
Leave impressions on my mind deep

It's a traveller's delight to walk by the silent streams
Looking at the tall trees and the lush green grasses
A true nature lover's delight, indeed!
Spotting a butterfly with its divine design fluttering
In the picture perfect setting is a dream come alive

It never tires me to walk on the velvety grasses
In those peaceful moments time never passes
With rays of the sunlight like God's benevolent eyes
Falling on a wintry morning as cold as ice

The songs of the birds is music to the ears

Unlike the cacophony of the world we hear
Everything in nature has rhythm and rhyme
Like the mystery of the falling rain, unravelling with
time

21. A Friend
(Inseparable part of life)

What you can do no one can do
Ever wondered why the universe made you?

You sacrifice your comfort without giving a thought
Can there ever be anyone like you? I think not!

You create a moment special for me
When you are just there with eyes filled with glee

You and me sew the memories together with the thread
of love
That leaves me with no words but to cherish the
blessings from above

You give meaning to my life; you make my day
May roses be always spread on your way

When you need me I will always be there
Because I know you need someone to care

I know it is hard but if we ever part ways
Let only be the bodies - my heart always prays

www.ingramcontent.com/pod-product-compliance
Lightning Source LLC
Chambersburg PA
CBHW050953030426
42339CB00007B/381

* 9 7 8 1 8 0 7 1 5 1 3 6 2 *